Thinking Outside the Box

LIFE'S LESSONS LEARNED
from
MIRACLES WITH MEANINGS

by
Virginia and Ralph Shotwell

Dear One,

Maybe you will know a bit more of miracles.?

Thank you so much for you do inspire me.

Virginia Shotwell

Wordclay
1663 Liberty Drive, Suite 200
Bloomington, IN 47403
www.wordclay.com

First published by Wordclay on 2/3/2008.

ISBN: 978-1-6048-1071-4

Printed in the United States of America.

This book is printed on acid-free paper.

The Dedication

TO JOANN

Early in your life,
We knew that you would go far;
And nothing would keep you
From grasping your star.

Superb mental gifts you've used,
Your caring heart too;
Those from justice removed
Have found you true blue.

As attorney, wife and mother
You are the best;
And with you as a daughter,
We surely are blessed.

The Contents

The Foreword

"Miracles are not contrary to nature,
but only contrary to what we know about nature."
-- St. Augustine

"A wise man should consider that health is
the greatest of human blessings,
and learn how by his own thoughts
to derive benefit from his illnesses."
-- Hippocrates

A miracle has been defined as a divinely natural phenomenon experienced humanly as the fulfillment of spiritual law. Each day, millions of miracles occur. We are among the fortunate who have recognized some of the events in our lives to be miracles. We also have been blessed by the lessons we have learned from these events.

This book has been written in the hopes that the insights shared will be helpful to you, the reader. We do not consider ourselves unique, and we hope you will not do so. Indeed, most likely you could share information on even greater miracles in your life or in the lives of others.

We have appended some of our poems which are on subjects treated earlier in the book. All of them have appeared in previous publications, some of them in several. Also, some have received recognitions and awards in poetry-writing contests.

Virginia and Ralph Shotwell

CHAPTER ONE
Doctors Did Their Best; God Did The Rest

Virginia Lambeth Shotwell

My birth was a miracle because I was trapped in the birth canal when all contractions stopped. The doctor, using forceps, tried and tried to hook my forehead at the eye sockets, finally pulled me down the birth canal. That was in New York City. At age 11, I moved, with my parents, to Richmond Virginia. It was there that I married Ralph Shotwell, another University of Richmond graduate. We were to live first in Rochester, New York while he was a student at Colgate Rochester Divinity School, then in Richmond while he was on the religion department's faculty and director of campus religious activity at the University, and then again in Rochester while he was senior pastor of Greece Baptist Church. It was in Rochester that other miracles occurred in my life.

At 31 years of age, I was diagnosed with acute nephritis. Both kidneys were functioning only at ten-percent. The year was 1957 when I was sent home from the hospital for complete bed rest. Seven doctors agreed that an additional complication was posed by my early pregnancy and that, because I could not live long enough to bring the child to birth, the fetus would have to be aborted. I did not want this done because it would have been acceptable to me to die with my child. The procedure was scheduled for the next morning. I prayed that I would be told whether or not it should be canceled. Early the next morning, a screen appeared on a blank wall of my hospital room. I walked into the picture and realized I was carrying a baby in my arms. Continuing to walk down a long corridor with no doors, I reached the end where a blinding light stunned me and I was left standing alone. A psychiatrist later told me that I had taken my baby down the birth canal and given it up even before the procedure was scheduled. I do know that the vision made me realize I should have the abortion. My two daughters needed me to be with them.

The doctors also advised my husband that I should be constantly medicated with penicillin and otherwise made as comfortable as possible. Further, he was told he should expect my death within a few months. At that time, there were neither dialysis treatments nor transplants.

A Quaker friend recommended some books, two of which were on spiritual healing and meditation. Having been raised in Christian Science, I always believed that with God all things are possible. The readings confirmed this belief and also aided my movement into deeper meditation.

I was able to totally release my daughters, then 4 and 6 years-old, to God's care because I knew the Love of God was all any of us needed. I had been arrogant to think that my love for them was great than God's. This was a turning point in my recovery. After one year in bed, healing of the kidney linings was accelerated and seven years later it was complete. Even earlier, when the penicillin therapy was terminated, the doctor said that if I had a sore throat the medication should be reinstated immediately. My response was: "In that case, I will not have another sore throat." For over fifty years, I have not. I came to believe that each cell and atom of our bodies knows its function and produces its desired effect until a traumatic event or new mind-set makes it react in an "unnatural" way.

Fourteen years after this illness, I was teaching social studies full-time in Quirk Middle School in Connecticut. We had moved there as Ralph became the senior pastor of Hartford's Central Baptist Church.

The Yale Medical School asked me to donate my kidneys for research after my death. I have arranged for this, knowing that the researchers will find the kidneys are stronger than they would have been, just as bones that repair themselves are stronger at that point.

My other Rochester miracle involved many broken bones. At age 41, after returning from a family camping trip, I was carrying twenty books which needed to be returned to the library. Wearing

10

new shoes, I crossed our blacktop driveway where there was an oil slick. I suddenly stepped to one side as my right knee crashed hard into my left ankle, crushing it and breaking both bones in my leg. I prayed that I would not pass out from the excruciating pain as Ralph rushed me to the hospital emergency room. There we learned that an orthopedist with excellent credentials was already in the hospital treating another patient. We agreed that he be consulted.

In the hallway outside my room, the doctor showed Ralph the X-ray results. He did not want me to know the results until after he set the bones. My left ankle was totally shattered, with splintered bones scattered around the area, and the left leg was broken in two places. He explained that, with the absence of two inches of bone structure, the leg would be shorter than the other one, resulting in my walking flat-footed and with a limp. Worse yet was the fact that the many tiny bones would tend to shift and future surgeries would be necessary to remove them from where they lodged. He added that I probably would never be free of pain.

I accepted a pain killer because of the almost unbearable pain, but demanded that I be conscious as the bones were set. I also gave permission for two interns to assist the doctor. He then looked me in the eyes and said: "I promise you I will do the very best I can." My reply was: "You do that, and God will do the rest!"

The complicated procedure involved the lifting of my foot away from the socket, the pulling of it down to bring it forward beyond my ankle. An intern held the leg and another the foot while the doctor positioned it into the right place. He then cupped his free hand around the area of the ankle and collected as many of the splintered bones as he could.

I was checked into the hospital for overnight to await surgery early the next morning. After setting the broken leg bones, he would have to insert a pin in the ankle but would not know where to position it until other X-rays were taken.

When the doctor entered my room the next morning, he did

not look well. My first thought was "He is not going to operate on me today!" but I did not say that. I only asked how he felt. He responded, in reference to the new X-rays: "Apparently there's been some mistake. We shall have to take still other X-rays." I went to radiology, had another set of X-rays made, but they only confirmed the previous set. There was no need for surgery—no need for a pin. Every bone was in place. I recovered to walk without a limp. My legs are the same length. I am not flat-footed. There has been no further pain.

The doctors did their best, at the time of my birth, my nephritis, and my broken bones; God did the rest! I am thankful to the doctors who were God at work, and to God!

CHAPTER TWO
Born, Again And Again

J. Ralph Shotwell

Virginia shared the miracle of her birth. Miracles have also attended my birth and several rebirths.

I was born prematurely at seven months. This occurred at home where incubators and other technology now used for preterm births were not available. My small body had to be carried on a pillow until it fully developed. There were many predictions that I would die. Miraculously, I did not.

There were later predictions that I was dying. In early childhood, I developed double pneumonia. My father wrapped me in several blankets and drove me in an unheated car over snow and ice filled roads some thirty miles from our home in Brookneal, a small town in southwestern Virginia, to the nearest hospital. There they did what was then usual and packed me in ice.

The hospital had a practice that when it was thought a patient was dying, all the medical personnel on the patient's floor gathered around the bed, held hands and prayed. When I had not come out of a prolonged coma, they instituted the practice. Much to their surprise and joy, in the midst of their praying I came to life and greeted them.

It was shortly thereafter that I publicly professed my Christian Faith, joined the town's Baptist Church, and announced that I wanted to be a candidate for the Christian ministry. Surely, I did not know at that early age all that would be involved in these commitments. Indeed, each new day has been a learning experience requiring many recommitments.

Virginia has written of our ministries in Richmond, Rochester, and Hartford. Before these, I was the pastor of Union

Avenue Baptist Church in Paterson, New Jersey, and after these I was the senior pastor of Flossmoor Community Church in suburban Chicago, Illinois, and later still the Executive Director of the International Council of Community Churches.

It was while I was at the Flossmoor Church that a series of miracles occurred. Intense stomach pains resulted in the diagnosis of appendicitis, a rush to the hospital, and surgery revealing that the appendix had burst, poison had spread throughout my body, and there was peritonitis or inflammation of the membrane lining the abdominal cavity. Not expecting me to live, the surgeon, whenever he later saw me, called me his "miracle patient".

I was placed in extreme isolation, but at home. It was believed that the risk of further infection could best be avoided there, rather than in the hospital. Although recovery was considered doubtful, doctors believed that it was dependent upon the drainage of the massive amounts of accumulated poisonous fluids. There was fever for twenty-eight days before such began. Although recovery was very slow, and although during the process extreme physical weakness occurred, it eventuated. There then followed bouts with phlebitis or inflammation of the leg veins, emboli or blood clots in the legs. and a life-threatening grand mal seizure. There was ample opportunity in all of this for me to learn life-changing lessons.

Other miracle-and-lesson-filled experiences occurred more recently during retirement years. In 1981, at the age of 65, I retired from the executive position with the International Council of Community Churches even though, during three different nine-month periods, I returned to that organization for an interim assignment, and also accepted such an assignment with two other church organizations servicing churches on a national scale. In retirement, we maintained residences in Florida and also first in Illinois and then in Massachusetts.

It was in Florida that I suffered from pericarditis or inflammation of the membrane surrounding the heart. This lining was completely destroyed, and while certain interim precautions were necessary, in seven years complete restoration occurred.

It was in Massachusetts that illnesses occurred from which, at this writing, I am continuing to recover. The first relates to my eyesight. During early childhood, I believed that everyone had sight similar to mine until a sixth grade teacher taught me otherwise. At her insistence, and with my mother's help, I secured corrective glasses for my extreme nearsightedness. The optometrist advised that I forget about continuing my education beyond high school, since he predicted that by age 20 I would be blind.

I reasoned that I would rather be an educated blind person than an uneducated seeing one, so I not only graduated from college but also from seminary, and other post-graduate institutions, and earned a total of four academic degrees. At age 80, I still have good eyesight, thanks to the care given by a succession of other optometrists and retinal specialists. The first in this succession determined that my nearsightedness was due to a weakened condition in my eyes traceable to my premature birth, and to the fact that my mother lost her first child at birth when she had measles. He prescribed less help from the lenses and also exercises, designed to strengthen the eyes. While wearing glasses, I had tunnel vision. Great improvement, including side vision, eventuated when it was possible for me to wear contact lenses. Clearest vision occurred following cataract surgery and the implanting of lenses.

At age 50, it was discovered that I had the dry type of macular degeneration in both eyes. At age 80, the degeneration in the right eye had become the more dangerous wet type. While there was no guarantee of positive results, two shots of a drug only recently available were injected into the eye. A third shot was planned but, upon examination, the surgeon pronounced that it was unnecessary. The bleeding of the retinal veins had ceased, the damaged tissue had been repaired, and my vision was the best ever. Both he and we readily pronounced it miraculous.

When experiencing illness of any type, it is natural for one to hope and pray for a return to the pre-illness condition. So often, in my experiences, there was not a return to the past but a giant leap into the future.

One of my favorite words is futalgia. You will not find it in a dictionary. I have coined it. It is the opposite of nostalgia, a fond longing for that which was. Combining a part of the word nostalgia with a part of the word future, we have futalgia, a fond longing for that which is better than the past. In illness, as in any crisis, we need to engage in futalgic hope and prayer.

Shortly after the wet macular degeneration was discovered, I experienced the first of three emergency-laden hospitalizations because of acute deep venous thrombosis. Blood clots formed in the lungs and double pneumonia developed, as well as other complications. As the causes were uncertain, doctors began calling me their "mystery patient". While, as in previous blood clotting, coumadin therapy was prescribed, during the third hospitalization a team of researchers determined that this blood thinner was causing rather than preventing the clotting. They, by way of scores of tests, arrived at the opinion that I had either inherited or acquired the antiphospholopib antibody which causes clotting and is unresponsive to coumadin. I am now receiving, and predictably for the remainder of my life I will receive, daily shots of another thinner, recently approved lovenox.

I was expected to die at least twice during these hospitalizations. I did not, but the toll on my physical wellbeing was such that three weeks in a rehabilitation center for physical and occupational therapies were necessary.

Shortly following release from the center, I was rushed for a fourth time to the hospital because of internal hemorrhaging. Within eight hours, without any surgical treatment, the bleeding miraculously ceased and tests revealed no evidence of any ruptured organ. It was surmised that the bleeding could have been caused by a flare-up of diverticulitis. During one night, my intensive care nurse awakened me with the statement that I had to be kept awake and also have additional blood transfusions, otherwise I would die. My blood pressure had been reduced to 50 over 13.

I have deliberately chosen "Born, Again And Again" rather than "Death, Again And Again" as this chapter's heading. You will understand my reasoning when in a later chapter I share some details of a particular rebirth.

CHAPTER THREE
Lessons Learned:
Move Beyond Darkness Into Light

"Every tomorrow has two handles.
We can take hold of it with
the handle of anxiety or the handle of faith."
-- Unknown

"To believe with certainty, we must begin with
doubting."
-- Stanislaw Leszczynski

The Spirit comes to me in dreams. The most impressive spiritually focused dreams come in a group of three. While I was ill in bed with the nephritis explained earlier, I dreamed I was in ancient Egypt where I had been laid in a stone sepulcher deep inside a pyramid. The first two nights I woke up from the dream in a cold sweat so glad to find that I had escaped being buried alive. The third night I was in the stone sepulcher with the heavy stone again covering the top. This night, however, I went through the stone and out. When I awoke, I knew I could live beyond death and had the assurance that it was absolutely nothing but passing from one realm to another. This was when the deterioration stopped and healing began. Later I found out from a Coptic scholar that this is the 30th test in the Egyptian priesthood.

My spiritual encounter was my dark night of the soul. It was like being in a dream, but this was completely real. I was in a charred black-black forest-like place where the black mud kept sinking as I tried to lift each foot and then leg, until I went into the black quicksand and was swallowed up inch-by-inch until only my nose and mouth were above the surface. Then nothing. I was nothing; God was nothing. Time ceased. I awakened and sat down in the next room. It was then that a force like a bolt of lightning went through my body from head to toe. The next minute gigantic weights went off my shoulders. I looked over my left shoulder to see if someone was there. No one was there; I was alone yet I almost saw the shadow of a head near the door jam. I asked who it was, but it disappeared. For a week I was filled with great joy and felt that my feet did not even touch the ground.

I have been most fortunate in that I was raised in Christian Science. I never understood sin, evil, and why someone died for me so long ago. My spiritual life had Jesus' teachings as a guide for right living. I cannot remember any time in my life that God and I were not together and co-partners. I guess this is my spiritual journey: I Am+i am=One.

-- *Virginia*

---000---

Virginia has been of immense help to me in the embracing of some teachings of the ancient metaphysical religions. In addition to an accomplished career in education as a secondary school teacher, a college and university professor, and coordinator of a career education center, she is a licensed spiritual counselor in Religious Science International.

Our research has documented that most if not all of the God-centered world religions contain elements of metaphysical theology. For example, the oneness of God. Did not the Apostle Paul advise that there is one God of us all, who is above all, through all, and in all?

Even as I publicly professed my Christian Faith, I had some doubts about some of the teachings and practices perpetrated in some of its institutions. This doubt continued into seminary to such an extent that I engaged in much soul-searching questioning of my commitment to ministry. Indeed, certain of that school's faculty planted some doubt in me. One of them often quoted Alfred Lord Tennyson to the effect that "there lives more faith in honest doubt than in half the creeds." Others led me to understand that doubt is necessary to "thinking outside the box" and to growing in the development of a meaningful and lasting faith. I was encouraged to keep doubt and faith in a relevant tension when my mother, the major source of my early understanding of God, confided that she, too, wrestled with doubt.

During some of my earlier described illnesses, doubt became as mentally painful as the physical suffering. Often I was anxious about both the present and the future, agonizing over the presence or absence of God, the adequacy or inadequacy of the medical caregivers, the helpfulness or futility of the seeming unending testings and procedures, the eventual outcome with its life-changing possibilities, and of much importance, the ways in which Virginia and our daughters were being or could be negatively affected.

I had many "dark nights of the soul" but the application of the metaphysical mind-over-matter principle was of great help as I, thankfully, passed through those nights and into the light of new days of faith.

-- *Ralph*

CHAPTER FOUR
Lessons Learned:
Believe And See

**"Faith is to believe what you do not see;
the reward of this faith is to see what you believe."
-- St. Augustine**

**"We have grown in science and technology;
now we will grow in consciousness.
This will be the greatest growth of all,
making the rest of our advances
look insignificant by comparison."
-- Unknown**

When illness results in mental and physical weakness, it is easy to feel hopeless, and discouragement can quickly blossom into depression. This is especially so when, as was the case in my most recent illness, you have to adjust to being completely dependent upon others. For examples, it is both humbling and humiliating to have others bathe you, and especially to have them clean you when you are not in control of bowel movements.

While it is difficult to see yourself in such a sad state and muster the hope for improvement, I learned that I had to deliberately attempt, as a song popular in my generation advised, to accentuate the positive and eliminate the negative. Or as Helen Keller advised, I tried to keep my face to the sunshine so I could not see a shadow.

For too many years, scientifically oriented persons challenged faith-oriented persons with such statements as "Show me proof and then I will believe" or "Seeing is believing." More recently, scientific research has allowed the reverse to be said, namely "Believing is seeing."

I found it possible to concentrate on short term improvements, to picture the improvement desired within an hour or a day, to believe that the improvement would occur, and offer prayers of gratitude to God for the gift. For examples: "I thank you, God, for the strength to stand this pain until it is possible for me to have the next pain-relieving medication." "I accept with gratitude that I will be able to do what is required of me in the next laboratory test." "I praise you, God, that I will be able to get out of bed without help... that I will be able to take my first steps without support."

I also found it helpful to envision and offer prayers of thanksgiving for improvement needed in other patients in the hospital and rehabilitation center; likewise for my many caregivers. While there is truth in Voltaire's statement that the art of medicine consists in amusing the patient while nature cures the disease, I was very much aware, and extremely appreciative, of the ways in which God ministered to me through the doctors and nurses. There were times when tiredness invoked by long hours and short staffing characterized their presence. I was also thankful that so many in these professions were open to alternative medical procedures, and that Virginia is an accomplished practitioner of Reiki, an energy transferal therapy.

In all of my illnesses, Virginia has been and still is my primary caregiver. It has pained me greatly to observe the tiredness occasioned in her by her frequent and long visits to the hospitals, and her having to do the myriad of necessary things I would have normally done or joined her in doing. Often I feared for her health. So, it will not surprise you when I say that I prayed for her, just as most surely she very effectively prayed for me.

The author of the Bible Book of James said that prayers offered in faith will heal the sick. I believe that my healings have eventuated because of the prayers of my wife and our daughters, my brothers and sisters-in-law, and the hundreds of friends that we have been privileged to make throughout this and many other nations.

-- *Ralph*

---000---

Learning to live intuitively, that is, as a co-creator with the Universal Mind, has six steps: (1) Meditate and learn to listen to the still small voice within you. Open yourself to the Knowing. Say to yourself in a given situation,"I know there is within me the Spirit that knows what I need, and I now receive it." (2) Seek only to know the best and the highest, for this is the Truth for you that you really want. (3) Watch for guidance in any form: coincidence, sychronicity, dreams, ideas that keep recurring in your thoughts. (4) Be patient. (5) Accept and trust the value of what you receive and give thanks. (6) Visualize and know it is already here.

When will I know I have achieved intuition? (1) It feels right (peace). You will be at the center of the spiritual circle where there is no movement. All happens around you but you are in the perfect place. (2) The test of intuition is that love is the base. (3) Signs and wonders follow and you are in the flow of your good.

Peace is like smiling repose—total contentment and trust in the Divine as each moment unfolds.

-- *Virginia*

CHAPTER FIVE
Lessons Learned:
Embrace The Greatest

**"Being deeply loved by someone gives you strength;
loving someone deeply gives you courage."
-- Lao Tzu**

**"You, yourself, as much as anybody
in the entire universe, deserve your love."
-- Buddha**

Remembering the long debates we had in college classes about what affected a person's life more, heredity or environment, I always concluded that both had very significant effects, but the primary part of the whole equation is not which is dominant but what beliefs were learned from each of them.

As I think of my early rearing, two very different admonitions rise to the forefront. The first is "Love is not what you say but what you do." The second is "You should love other people, not yourself." I was told that otherwise I would be a very selfish person. Because of these instructions, it took me until young adulthood to realize I should not just like myself and who I was, but I needed to love myself more so I could pass it on to others. Works of love and charity are wonderful goals. Yet, words and expressions of appreciation and love are also very important, and especially to those who might not know your thoughts until they are spoken. As I am able to forgive myself for my wrong beliefs, I am freed to understand and forgive others more.

The most common denominator in all of living is that when thought and belief change, new birth results.

Other college class discussions were on Darwin's theory of the survival of the fittest. This is such a belligerent idea. I much prefer to think that, as we emerged, there was more of a cooperative experience which would have caused a symbiotic coexistence.

This mutual interdependence becomes evident during times of illness. While I was bedridden with nephritis and unable to provide certain care for my husband and daughters, I was thankful for the help provided by volunteers in our church family and by a professional caregiver whose services we were able to secure. Volunteer help can also be available within one's residential neighborhood. Most often, this is on other than an organized basis. Meadowbrook Village into which we moved when first residing in Massachusetts has a system for providing caring help which Ralph and I organized.

A caregiver is usually one within the patient's immediate family. Available self-help books, support groups, and on-line chat rooms provide advice on ways in which a caregiver can not only care for the ill person but also care for one's self. Loving and caring for one's own self is a necessary ingredient in loving and caring for another.

I learned, while caring for Ralph in our home following his hospitalizations, that the benefits a caregiver receives are sensitivity, patience, understanding, empathy and alert attentiveness. I also found that humor is of great help in maintaining a positive attitude.

-- *Virginia*

---oOo---

It is easy for one at any time, and especially during illness, to become self-centered and even selfish. Feeling sorry for oneself can cause one to expect sympathy from everyone else. It requires a great deal of courage and will-power to move beyond this devastating attitude into one with more positive results.

During my adult illnesses, I engaged in much reflection on my past action and inaction in relationships with others, especially family and close friends. There is no perfect human being. Therefore each of us has made and will make mistakes. What to do with them? We should admit and regret them. If we fail to do this, our credibility suffers, especially when there is proving evidence. We should undo them if possible. If not, we should do that which will keep any resulting harm to a minimum. Then we should guard against making the same or similar mistakes again.

I seriously wondered if I had done what was best in subjecting my wife and daughters to sacrifices inherent in the "fishbowl" or "glasshouse" type of existence typical in clergy homes, and to the hardships resulting from many years of low salaries typically paid clergy. Moves to new pastorates occasioned painful disruptions in my wife's career and in our daughters' schooling and friendships.

This reflection prompted conversations in which Virginia, Donna Lynn, and JoAnn, in expressing love for me, attempted to assure me that the best choices were made, given the knowledge then possessed and conditions then existing. Whether or not this was correct, the confronting of these and similar matters always resulted in earnest desires for time beyond the illnesses in which I could increase my acts of love for them and others.

The love that others have provided me became most notable during my illnesses. I have never doubted that Virginia loves me. Throughout our now more than sixty years of marriage, she has provided the prime example of translating love into action. And, as the Talmud teaches, deeds of love and kindness are equal in weight to all the commandments. While our bonding has always been strong, it became even stronger during her and my illnesses.

Our older daughter, Donna Lynn, had burdens of her own. For more than thirty years before her death, she struggled with a bipolar illness. We attempted to show her love and provide the kind of caring that would not prevent her from living up to her capabilities. She, with her limitations, showed us love and caring, and especially during the last seven years of her life, the bonding was very rewarding.

Like her mother, our younger daughter, JoAnn, believes that love is shown not only in words but also in actions. As an accomplished attorney, she has been of untold help to us in situations requiring her expertise. For example, in my recent illness, she handled some of the negotiations with hospital and insurance personnel – responsibilities beyond my capabilities, given my weakened mental and physical condition, and responsibilities that did not have to be added to Virginia's already extensive ones. Her husband, George, was also of much appreciated help, especially as our residence had to be fitted with some equipment necessary for my return there.

This is probably the place that I should insert the fact that, while my hospital experiences revealed much that is right about our national health system, they also revealed much that is wrong. For instances, the seemingly endless and at least partly repetitive and thus unnecessary questionings and recordings that are burdensome to the ill persons and their families; the obvious absence of needed communications or the presence of incorrect communications among medical personnel and between them and the insurance personnel, the ill persons and their families; and the incorrect billings which complicate recovery times. To repeat, JoAnn's handling of some of these matters has been very helpful. Opportunities for bonding with her and her family have been increased as we have resided a part of each year in Massachusetts, the state where she lives.

My reflections have often involved my now deceased parents. My father, bedridden in his last year because of a stroke, had loving care from my mother which resulted in a more mature bonding between the two of them than had existed previously. When I last visited him, I verbally expressed my love for him, as I had many times before. For the first time he said that he loved me. The conversation that ensued resulted in a bonding that we had never before experienced. I never doubted that my mother loved me. She demonstrated this in so many ways. I believe that she never doubted my love for her. The last time I verbalized it was when she was in a coma, resulting from an aneurism from which she never recovered. I did not hesitate to speak with her. For a reason which I will share later in the book, I know that persons in comas can hear that said.

Because we have resided in so many states, our friends are many and geographically widespread. For example, when we observed the fiftieth anniversary of our wedding, we had to plan celebrations in four different locations. Reflections during illnesses have not only allowed renewed appreciation and concern for friends, but also have prompted increased concern over the needs of millions of humans, in ever-widening circles, around the world.

Three Greek words can be translated into English as "love": eros, philia, and agape. Ancient Greeks used eros in speaking of how persons can be attracted to each other because of the attractive physical qualities they possess. They used philia to reference how persons can be attracted and even bound to each other because of common interests, shared goals. Agape was reserved for use in communicating the belief that there can be a continual bonding between persons even when attractive physical, mental and spiritual qualities are temporarily replaced by some not-so-attractive ones; even when common interests and shared goals are temporarily replaced by divergent and even divisive ones.

These are among the qualities of agape: open-mindedness, understanding, tolerance, forgiveness, caring, helpfulness, hopefulness, patience and perseverance. The hatred existing in our intimate interpersonal relationships and in our worldwide relationships needs to be replaced with an agape kind of love. Further, this love must begin at the most personal of levels since one can properly love others only when there is proper love for one's own self.

Jesus, when asked about the greatest commandment, taught that we are to love God with the whole of our being, and then love our neighbor with the same intensity as we love ourselves. When asked who the neighbor might be, he identified such as anyone in need.

Throughout the centuries, sages have advised that even possessors of great knowledge and faith, if devoid of agape, are incomplete persons. For example, the Apostle Paul said that of faith, hope and love, the latter is the greatest.

A lesson to be learned in times of both good and bad health is that love should be embraced.

-- Ralph

CHAPTER SIX
Lessons Learned:
Set Priorities

**"Failure doesn't occur when
you do not reach your goal,
but when you do not have a goal to reach."
-- Unknown**

**"Life is not having and getting,
but being and becoming."
-- Matthew Arnold**

In the Chinese language, the same characters are used in spelling the word "crisis" and the word "challenge". A challenge of crisis is to not look back in anger or forward in fear, but to look around in awareness. Illnesses provide opportunities for becoming aware of unimportant and unneeded elements that have crowded our living, and to rid ourselves of them. Likewise, opportunities for becoming aware of life's important and needed elements, and with an attitude of gratitude, enjoy the good that is in the now.

I am fond of the word "darshanic". You will not find it in any English dictionary. It is a Hindi word, related to the Hindu religion. A darshanic individual is one embracing the truth that reality consists of various contexts, one who climbs, rung by rung, the ladder of increasingly higher levels of consciousness, and thus comes to possess new perspectives and priorities.

Illnesses provide opportunities for establishing or reordering personal priorities, and setting them within the context of a renewed understanding of one's principles or values. They can be related to unfinished tasks or newly embraced ones.

Personal documents such as birth, marriage and death certificates, divorce or separation decrees, naturalization and military records should be readily available. Likewise, mortgages, house deeds, auto titles, and up-to-date insurance, financial and income tax records. Written instructions relative to burial or cremation arrangements or desires should be reviewed annually. Likewise, those documents relative to a medical or health power of attorney, a living will, the durable power of an attorney, and a living trust.

When Virginia and I began to travel extensively, especially on an international scale, our primary care physician insisted that we keep as complete as possible medical histories. He and successive physicians have always supplied copies of any lab tests, and sometimes copies of notes made in office visits. Most hospitals have been cooperative in these matters. In order to obtain cooperation from others, it has been necessary to voice reminders that such records are the property of the patient. Since it is now known that many illnesses are inherited, a medical history should include information on those in one's blood family.

During my illnesses in adulthood, I thought much about what was unfinished in these mentioned tasks, and hoped for time in which I could accomplish that which would lessen the burdens of Virginia and our daughters.

I have also thought about what I might still do toward a more complete application and realization of the principle of unity among humankind. It is a principle I have sought to protect and promote in the whole of my ministry, giving leadership in interfaith endeavors at local, national and international levels. Further, Virginia and I have been blessed as we have visited in 116 different nations, many of them several times, including preaching and consultative missions, and study tours. Having taught comparative religions, we welcomed contacts with persons in many God-centered world religions, regretted evidences that religion has been misused by some to effect division and devastation, and rejoiced over evidences that religion has correctly motivated unity and peace with justice.

Our experiences in various world cultures, and with persons of all ages, genders, races, and sexual orientations, have increased our desire that the worth, dignity and equality of each person be acknowledged, and each person's right of individual conscience be assured. These experiences have also increased our appreciation of the richness of diversity and our belief that it is unity without uniformity that we must seek. Among our highest goals has been to be as inclusive as the love of God.

While I have always considered Jesus to be a sufficient guide for the kind of living intended by God, I have not considered him to be the only God-provided guide. To believe otherwise is to attempt to limit a limitless God.

Truth has many sides; truth is multi-faceted. No one person can possess the whole truth. It can only be hoped that at any point-in-time, one is progressing toward an increased and more inclusive understanding of truth. Different portions of the truth progressively possessed by different persons, societies, cultures, and religions need to be shared for the common good.

My first international travel was to gather information on and provide evaluations of mission stations. I was profoundly impressed by those in which the major goals had not to do with conversions to the Christian religion but with the meeting of human need for food, clothing, shelter, health care, and education. I was especially appreciative of the help being given refugees in Hong Kong who, at the time, were daily fleeing Communist China by the thousands. The mission stations we visited there were sponsored by the USA-based, interdenominational Church World Service.

Shortly after these experiences, I became the senior pastor of Central Baptist Church in downtown Hartford, Connecticut. With the cooperation of its concerned membership and the memberships of other nearby churches, and in coordination with area businesses and governmental agencies, we established many helping services: an academy providing secretarial training and procuring employment for women seeking escape from welfare; studios for artists who, for reduced rent, were willing to accept interns from

35

inner city schools; programs for child care, youth tutoring, crisis counseling, alcohol and drug rehabilitation, and the special needs of the elderly. The desire to contribute even more in attempts to right social injustices provided me strong motivation to recover from some of my illnesses.

It was during my most recent illness that both Virginia and I began thinking about authoring this book. Our journalistic interests began when we were students in the University of Richmond in Virginia. She was editor-in-chief of a campus yearbook, and I was in such role with the campus newspaper. Both she and I have authored professional books and contributed articles to professional magazines. I have edited newspapers for several religious organizations and had non-sectarian inspirational articles published in other newspapers. We realized that the goal of publishing a book of this nature would be a different undertaking. We hoped it would be one helpful to others, and indeed would assist in my recovery.

Anyone can get old. All you have to do is live long enough. However, some of my thoughts during my most recent illness had to do with more than getting old. They had to do with growing old, with the emphasis on growing. One can do nothing and still get old. On the other hand, at whatever age, one can utilize in each day some of the many opportunities to grow. While this will not reverse the aging process in the physical body, the mental and spiritual advances will slow the process. Further, it will provide energy and enthusiasm needed for the years remaining in the physical body, and will be a reflection of life beyond the physical body.

-- *Ralph*

---000---

When persons think of aging, negative things come to mind, such as illness, disability, or loss of independence. Others think of aging as retirement, time for family, time to develop new interests and possibly travel more.

Living one's life to the fullest, no matter what the changes, is the only way to go. Being stuck in the past should not be the reason for not taking risks, for not trying something new. We note that, during younger years, if we did not take risks we did not grow.

A wise man in his nineties said, "Being happy growing old is to have something pending." New goals and interests add enthusiasm and joy to an ordinarily routine day. Our minds are divinely designed to be active and creative. If we do not continue to use them in this manner, there will be no sense of well being. Living too much in the past gives rise to pessimism which could lead to illnesses and unhappiness, not to just to one but to others as well.

Some younger people seem older than those in their eighties. They think they are stuck in jobs they dread. They blame others for their difficulties. They have no goals to which they aspire. The bottom line on having youthful vitality and a happy productive life is to have one filled with purpose. The mind set with inner direction and commitment overcomes the result of circumstances.

While becoming more interested in aging, I asked friends and associates living in a retirement community what traits they felt were needed to maintain a youthful vitality regardless of age. There is no priority order for my findings.

First in my listing is flexibility. This means not getting stuck in old ways. It also includes making peace with the disappointments and tragedies that happen and moving beyond them.

Second is a positive attitude, hitchhiking on the first.

Third is a questioning mind that stays current, discussing events, books, and ideas. Many join book clubs, attend classes, and stretch their minds in other stimulating ways. Purpose and enthusiasm have great value to those who are working on projects, completing collections or continuing hobbies.

Fourth gets top priority. It is a good sense of humor. Their advice was to laugh as much as possible and not take oneself too seriously.

Fifth, exercise and good health habits maybe should have been mentioned earlier. They are essential for living well.

Sixth is gratitude for all the wonderful little things in nature and everyday associations with others.

Seventh is generosity. Those who contribute to the needs of others here and around the world are not only making a difference in the lives of others, but also in their own lives as they mature spiritually.

It is important to live each day to the fullest. Among the definitions of "young" is "the first stage of growth." The now moment, whatever your age, is the time for a new stage of growth. Youthful vitality will enhance that growth's continuance, as you age well and gracefully.

-- *Virginia*

CHAPTER SEVEN
Lessons Learned:
Laugh Often

"What soap is to the body, laughter is to the soul."
-- Yiddish Proverb

"A good laugh and a long sleep are the best cures in the
doctor's book."
-- Irish Proverb

A plaque which often hangs on the entrance door to our Massachusetts residence and a throw which we sometimes use in our Florida residence to warm us on its few cold days both contain these words: Live Well, Laugh Often, Love Much.

One's wellness is greatly dependent upon laughter. There is sound evidence that, by bringing balance to all the components of the immune system, it can help prevent diseases. Likewise, there is increasing proof that it can have a curative effect. It has been called by some "inside jogging".

In illness, it is easy to take everything and maybe everyone, especially one's own self, too seriously. Someone said that humor is despair refusing to take itself seriously.

So, whether ill or well, figure out what makes you laugh, and do it often. Surround yourself with laughing persons. Sharpen your joke telling skills. Share funny material, just as long as it is not at someone else's expense. More particularly, learn to laugh at and tell jokes on yourself.

Even though humor is a means of temporarily dulling pain, in many respects neither physical nor mental pain is a laughable matter. Painful loss comes in many forms: loss of a relative or friend in death; loss of a full life through physical, mental or emotional deterioration, loss of a job or otherwise lessening of economic well-being; losses associated with school, job or residence changes.

Loss comes in many forms, as does attendant grief. The stages of grief and their order vary from person to person. However, most often there is shock ("What?!", "Oh, No!"), disbelief ("There must be a mistake!", "Are you sure?"), questioning ("Why?", "Why me?, What at this time?, "Why in this way?), guilt ("What did I do wrong?", "What should I have done to prevent it?, and maybe bargaining (If I do this now, can it be changed?).

Virginia, one of the most positive thinking and acting persons I have ever known, often came to my hospital room equipped with humorous readings which eased my suffering. She also brought with her written materials used in her frequent meditations.

I vividly recall the times when she brought "Everyman's Search" authored by Rebecca Beard, one of the books recommended by our Quaker friend during Virginia's nephritis illness. When she prepared to read from it, the book opened repeatedly on a chapter in which Job, the Biblical character, is referenced.

Disaster after disaster fell upon Job. Some of his cattle were stolen; others were killed, as were his servants. His house was destroyed and his sons and daughters were killed in a windstorm. Then, he became seriously ill. Painful boils covered his entire body. His wife pleaded with him to renounce God and die. Even though his grief was great and his bewilderment greater, and even though he posed poignant questions to God, he labeled such pleading as foolish.

While Job had earlier known God intellectually, he awakened to a higher consciousness and began to seek God through the heart. He thus gradually sensed the reality of God's presence and love, leading him to the proclamation: "I know that my redeemer lives!"

Virginia told me that, in my stages of semi-consciousness, I could be heard quoting the twenty-third Psalm. This did not surprise me. Most often I have been able to hold firmly to my belief that God provides my every need, gives me strength, guides me in right paths, restores my spirit, gives me inner peace. Even when I am passing through such as "the valley of the shadow of death", God is with me. Indeed, I believe that I can never be separated from God's presence, goodness and love.

When increasingly we make real our love for God, ourselves and others, and when increasingly we gratefully accept the reality of God's love for all of us, our suffering will not be in vain and we will possess the good that can come from our pain, as did Job.

Live Well, Laugh Often, Love Much!

-- *Ralph*

---oOo---

When Ralph first asked me to marry him, I laughed. I did so because, knowing of his plans to enter the Christian ministry. I had reservations about being a clergy spouse. He then and later assured me that he was not asking me to be any church's minister of education. Instead, he was asking me to be his wife. Even though he supported me in being myself and not what some parishioners expected me to be, I experienced many challenges typical to most persons married to pastors. While he was the chief executive officer of The International Council of Community Churches, I was instrumental in founding and then coordinating a supportive international network of persons cast in roles such as mine.

Once while Ralph was meeting with a church's adults, and I was caring for the children, one of them suggested that we play wedding. Each of us volunteered for or was assigned a role. As "officiant", I asked the "bride" if she would take the "groom" as her

41

husband for better or worse. The girl quickly replied, "I'll take better." When asked if she would take him for richer or poorer, her response was, "I'll take richer." And you guessed it: to the question regarding sickness and health, she took health.

In a real sense, marriage is a matter of multiple choices. On a cruise, Ralph and I were the longest married couple among the passengers, or we were the ones willing to admit such. We were asked the secrets of a good marriage. In his joking mood, Ralph said that we had stayed together for so many years because he always allowed me to have the last word.

The question prompted a more serious exploration and a recommitment to two principles.

Kahlil Gibran, the mystic, wrote of the first. He advised that spaces are needed in a couple's togetherness. In other words, while marriage partners should possess certain beliefs together and pursue certain common interests, each should have the freedom of individuality. Gibran pictured oak and cypress trees, standing together but unable to grow in each other's shadow, the strings of a lute as being alone though they quiver with the same music, and two columns apart but supporting a structure. This writing of his was included in the readings at our sixtieth wedding anniversary service in which, as we had done on our fiftieth anniversary, we renewed our wedding vows.

Many marriage counselors have advised that marriage partners, above all else, need to be best friends. This is true of our relationship. We desire to be with each other more than anyone else, to enjoy such as the arts and travel together, to be supportive of each other in good and bad times, and to share things both great and small. Gibran said that it is in the dew of shared little things that the heart finds its morning and is refreshed.

Together, we laugh often and love much.

-- Virginia

CHAPTER EIGHT
Lessons Learned:
Fear Neither Life Nor Death

**"As a well-spent day brings happy sleep,
so life well used brings happy death."
-- Leonardo da Vinci**

**"What is mortal must be changed
into what is immortal;
what will die must be changed into what cannot die."
-- St. Paul**

When I was seven years old and in the third grade, I read a poem entitled "Suppose". I liked it so much that I copied it to take home. My mother saw it and asked if I wrote it. I said, "Yes." Later I found out that she had sent it to several relatives and praised me for my writing it. Only later did I find out what her question meant. She wanted to know if I composed it. I meant in my answer that it was my handwriting in cursive.

Supposing is probably my greatest gift. When I suppose greater possibilities, I am freed from limiting lesser ones.

Suppose that you and I are perfect spiritual beings with no limitations. We do not limit ourselves and we do not allow others to limit us by negative thinking, worries or wrong judgments, because we know that they have no part in and cannot alter our spiritual journey.

Suppose that sickness is lost in perfect health, ugliness is replaced with beauty, war with peace, fear with love, ignorance with truth, and darkness with light.

Suppose we decorate a tree of life with colorful lights of love expressing faith, hope, courage, conviction, passion, purpose, honor, humility, and forgiveness – all in joyful expressions.

Suppose there is a uniting drama in which principles, thoughts, purposes, teachings and motivations conspire to inspire the best productions ever. Suppose there are banners for beatitudes, centers for consciousness, companies for compassion, flags for forgiveness, governments for giving, libraries for love, monuments for mercy, schools for solitude, stadiums for spirit, temples for truth, and universities for unity.

Suppose this heaven on earth is a reality already because the most open hearts and the most marvelous minds have joined hands and eliminated physical pain, mental agony, emotional upsets and spiritual hunger. Come see this heaven with me.

Thinking makes it so. Let us bring this consciousness into true reality.

-- Virginia

---000---

"If We Only Have Love" by Jacques Brel became our family song after JoAnn was in the quartet that performed his musical in a college production. Her singing the song was a much appreciated highlight of the celebration of our sixtieth wedding anniversary.

Its words provide much meaning in our search for the good life on both sides of what is called death. The lessons it teaches are that, with love, there can be a better tomorrow in which the good we strive for on earth can eventuate. Further, that when we embrace love without fears we can sleep without tears, and that in love death has no shadow and that to be experienced beyond death will not be a foreign land.

Since life on each side of death has its mysteries, it is natural that we probe them with our questions. Sometimes we find at least partial answers; other times not. When one experiences existence outside one's physical body, as I have, certain questioning either ceases or at least lessens.

My experiences began long before I was capable of understanding any of their meanings. In the childhood experience with pneumonia, already explained, at some point while I was in the coma, my spirit separated from my physical body, observing it, seemingly lifeless, lying on the bed. Likewise, there was recognition of the presence and practice of those around the bed.

A similar out-of-body experience occurred later, in adulthood, when I had intense pain associated with a severely poisoned physical body, occasioned by the rupturing of the diseased appendix. It also has been referenced earlier. Almost daily for a lengthy period, when medication failed to provide needed relief, my spirit left my body and, feeling no pain, observed its torturous condition.

The most informative of my experiences began one morning at the breakfast table. I fainted. Virginia held my head while calling for help. As she led me to a bed, my disembodied spirit followed. I was conscious of persons gathering outside our home, of an arriving ambulance and paramedics, and of one of them informing the hospital that I would be dead on arrival. My spirit hovered over the ambulance enroute to the hospital, and knew that my notified physician awaited its arrival. Once I was on the examining table, my spirit entered a tunnel and traveled into a bright light. It was so lovingly and warmly inviting, I wanted to stay but was told I needed to return to my physical body.

Despite mythological writings, I observed in that light no "pearly gates", no "St. Peter's entrance examinations", no "judgment scales", no "golden streets". While I sensed the spiritual presence of my maternal grandfather, I did not see a physical presence.

My doctor later explained that he and others regarded me as clinically dead for at least ten minutes. I was diagnosed as having experienced a grand mal seizure. I was medicated for such, but only briefly because follow-up testing gave no evidence of such.

Have I experienced visits from those in life beyond death? Yes, as did my mother before me. I have been visited, for seemingly specific reasons, by my mother, father, daughter, niece, and a couple of dearly loved dogs. I have sensed the presence of these visitors in their physical bodies. It was my ascending spirit that sensed my grandfather's spiritual presence. Could it be that my physical self needed physical manifestations?

For many years, I was reluctant to speak of these out-of-body, near-death experiences. First, because in childhood they were beyond my understanding; then in adulthood, I feared they would be considered hallucinations. I have experienced hallucinations, especially during my recent illness. They were very hellish and frightening in nature. It was only during recovery that I was able to accept Virginia and JoAnn's understanding that they resulted from overly-strong pain medications.

Questions – I will always have them. However, given my experiential proof, I do not doubt that, just as life in my mother's womb was preparing me for life in this world, life in it has been preparing me for a peaceful, joyful, love-filled life in the world beyond this one.

-- *Ralph*

The Appendix

Poems by Virginia

FOR RALPH

God speaks to me
in the babbling of the brook,
in the volcano that shook,
in the guiding bird in flight,
in the sun setting at night.
Do you hear? I do.

God speaks to me
in the newborn baby's cry,
in the new rain's fresh reply,
in the tide held by the moon,
in a lover's step heard soon.
Did you hear? I did.

God spoke to me
in the fragrance of the rose,
in sermon messages you chose,
in the touch of caring hands,
in the beauty of our lands.
Did you know? I did.

God spoke again to me … spoke very personally:
You are perfect and complete,
and nothing will I delete.
You are always wholly mine,
greatly loved, truly divine.

GIFT OF GOD

God did not give me a burning bush
or tablets made of stone,
But just planted universal truths
to sprout for me alone.
Now I know this royal flush
is not of flesh or bone,
It is strength in solitude
placed here for me on loan.

WHAT IS LOVE?

Love puts music in laughter,
beauty in song,
warmth in a shoulder,
gentle in strong.

Love is magic in memories,
sunshine in skies.
gladness in giving,
starlight in eyes.

Love is fun in together,
sad in apart,
faith in tomorrow,
joy in a heart.

Love takes lumps from the throat,
tears from the eye,
aches from the loss,
darks from the sky.

Love is a mystery,
a message and a miracle
and the mastery
of the magnitude of life.

MOLDED MOMENTS

I spoke in my darkness and turned it to light,
Set stars, sun and moon as I varied day from night.

Who breathed into my spirit? An angel on this earth?
'Tis Spirit who created me, giving me eternal worth.

Great sages from on High were sent to torch the Light,
To glaze this earthen vessel with shining power bright.

It is the Potter who reshapes the beings of this land
Until the flow of heaven sparkles at each command.

These compassionate helpers spirit our infinity,
As Hands and Hearts perfect molded moments, eternally.

BEING ME

I am what's inside my skin.
Guess that is what I've always been.
Others see me at a glance
but don't know I'm in a trance—
I view myself from another stance.

In Reality I know it is from within
that I begin
to intertwine in Life Divine.

SHEDDING

A sudden loss causes moods to veer
because change is taking place.
There is a limbo time – some numbness
and some painful irritable growth.
Just like the snake that must shed
Its old exterior for the new skin,
I too must stop dragging the stale
Shreds and scales of my former life
to slither with surety up the steep slope
leaving the unneeded coffin behind.

Poems by Ralph

TO VIRGINIA

In your presence I know Faith;
To all that's true you aspire.

In your presence I know Hope;
All that is good you inspire.

In your presence I know Love;
The greatest gift to acquire.

In your presence I'll always be
Loving you through eternity.

THE ALL-IN-ALL

When Joseph left old Canaan land,
in the unknown he took his stand.

He thought the Lord he'd left behind,
but very soon he changed his mind.

Although we try to limit God,
the Divine's on each piece of sod.
In all of space and all of time,
The All-In-All reigns sublime.

In each created color and creed,
some of God's truth we see and heed.

ON VICTORY

What we called new was very old;
our discovery claims were much too bold.
While new land for us, it long had been
the home of others with different skin.

Persecuted, we did travel far;
freedom for us was the guiding star.
Then persecutors many became;
freed persons denied others the same.

We forced the cultures of other lands,
causing great harm with unjust demands.
On our religions we insisted,
ignoring truth that long existed.

Whenever prejudice is to be found,
there are not victors; victims abound.
Still victims can learn; its not too late!
Victors we'll become with love, not hate.

BEEN THERE, DONE THAT

My body I have left when pain persisted;
My Spirit was alive when death insisted.
Into the Light I went, its Love unending;
I now am back to make that Love extending.

PROOF

There are those who say proof must be objective.
I will dare to claim it can be subjective.
My experiences are sufficient for me.
I gladly share truth they allow me to see.

THE PATH UNENDING

The mountain is tall, the valley deep,
And the path I climb is very steep.

While at the bottom where anyone starts,
I learned that life has many parts.

Though the physical I thought of first,
I learned my body from my spirit burst.

Ere my body was, my spirit said,
"Let the body be for what's ahead."

Much needed knowledge has fed my mind;
While wisdom has been my spirit's find.

The Spirit from which my spirit came
Can see to it I'm reborn again.

Nothing will prevent my ascending
The mountain and the path unending.

TO LYNN

All night long I heard your cries,
"Dad, I hurt" you said.
As much in life dies,
your cries and hurts are now dead.

As old gave way to the new,
the bad to the good,
these words came from you:
"I'm here" and we understood.

Because The "I AM" is here,
we will not despair;
Our oneness is clear.
Rejoice! We're all in God's care.

Troubles beyond your control
plagued your days on earth;
Now in the Spirit World,
you will fulfill your true worth.

Love gave you birth and support;
Our love's with you still.
Peace for you fell short;
You have it now – it's God's will.

SPRING

A feeling of happiness throughout me
Comes only in Spring;
The thought of having a bird sing
Has just come to be.

The newly cut lawn
All grassy and green
Sets a beautiful scene
Like a sunrise at dawn.

The air so sweetly drifting,
The water flows gently by
Throwing pebbles as I lie –
It is a beautiful thing.

Flowers so bright
That peep up from the earth,
It's like having rebirth –
I can't resist the sight.

Winter is gone and Spring is here,
The sun is bright
And in the night
I dream that Summer is near.

Oh, but I wish it would never end
Observing a bird,
The things I've heard.
But next year's Spring God will send.

Blank page on reverse of last page of the appendix

Printed in the United States
208307BV00002B/328-345/P